BrAiN BENDERS

IT'S ONLY LOGICAL

Thanks to the creative team:

Senior Editor: Alice Peebles

Designer: Bryony Anne Warren and Collaborate Agency

First American edition published in 2015 by Lerner Publishing Group, Inc.

Hungry Tomato™
A division of Lerner Publishing Group, Inc.
241 First Avenue North
Minneapolis, MN 55401 USA

For reading levels and more information, look up this title
at www.lernerbooks.com.

Main body text set in Century Gothic STD 10/14.5
Typeface provided by Monotype.

Library of Congress Cataloging-in-Publication Data

Moore, Gareth, 1975–
    It's only logical / by Dr. Gareth Moore.
        pages cm. — (Brain benders)
        ISBN 978-1-4677-6346-2 (lb : alk. paper) — ISBN 978-1-4677-7203-7
(pb : alk. paper) — ISBN 978-1-4677-7204-4 (eb pdf)
        1. Logic puzzles. 2. Word games. I. Title.
    GV1493.M554 2015
    793.73   2015001587

Manufactured in the United States of America
1 – VP – 7/15/15

IT'S ONLY LOGICAL

by Dr. Gareth Moore

HUNGRY TOMATO™

MINNEAPOLIS

Contents

It's Only Logical

Are you a wizard with words? A ninja with numbers? It's time to show your skills with some numeric and word-based challenges.

You'll need to reason carefully to solve all the puzzles, but if you need help at any time just turn to the "Tips" section at the back of the book for some helpful hints. You can also check your answers and learn the secrets of each trick.

So put your thinking cap on and have fun!

Riddle me this

This is a simple riddle to get your brain working:

What occurs once in a minute, twice in a moment, but not once in a thousand years?

Need help with solving these puzzles? Turn to pages 26 – 28 for helpful tips.

Numbers and Reasoning

If you only know about math from school, you might think it's all hard work. But the truth is that math is full of interesting patterns and tricks, and numbers can be just as much fun to play with as anything else!

1 Tricks with numbers

Double your age, then add 6.

Okay!

Now divide the answer by 2 and subtract your age.

Done.

Would you be impressed if I knew the number you now have left? It's 3, isn't it?

Yes, that's amazing!

Can you figure out how this trick works by thinking about the math involved?

Here's another number trick! You could try it out on a friend.

- Think of a number between 1 and 9.
- Add 1 and multiply by 9.
- Add the digits together – for example, if you have 63, add 6 and 3 (to get 9).
- Now add 6 to the result.
- The number you have is 15!

Can you figure out why the answer is always 15?

2 Pouring problem

You have three water containers, each a different size.

Container **A** holds 3 quarts, container **B** holds 5 quarts, and container **C** holds 8 quarts.

A and **B** are both empty, but **C** is filled to the brim with 8 quarts of water.

How can you pour this water from one container to another so as to end up with exactly 4 quarts of water in both **B** and **C**?

Doing it by eye is not the answer – there is a precise, number-based method to use.

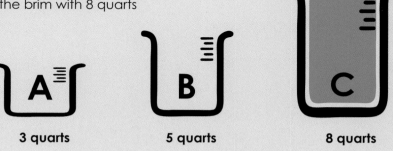

| 3 quarts | 5 quarts | 8 quarts |

3 River crossing

Can you solve this classic puzzle?

A man wants to cross a river with his dog, his cat, and a bowl of cat food. The problem is that he has to use a ferry to cross, and the ferryman will only let him bring one item across the river per trip. If he leaves the dog alone with the cat on either side of the river, the cat will get scared and run away. If he leaves the cat alone with the cat food, the cat will eat the food.

How can the man get all three across the river, without the cat either running away or eating the food? Can you figure out the correct sequence of ferry journeys?

Need help with solving these puzzles? Turn to pages 26 – 28 for helpful tips.

Number Manipulation

Are you good at solving number puzzles? On these pages you'll look for patterns in numbers, try some mathematical anagrams, and practice some of your mental arithmetic skills.

1 Number anagrams

By rearranging all these numbers and math symbols, can you figure out how to reach each of the given totals?

For example, you could make 17 by doing this: 2 x 5 + 7 = 17.

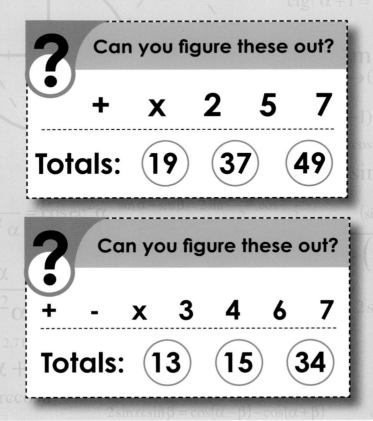

Can you figure these out?

+ x 2 5 7

Totals: (19) (37) (49)

Can you figure these out?

+ - x 3 4 6 7

Totals: (13) (15) (34)

2 Number sequences

Which number comes next in each countdown sequence? The first one is done for you as an example.

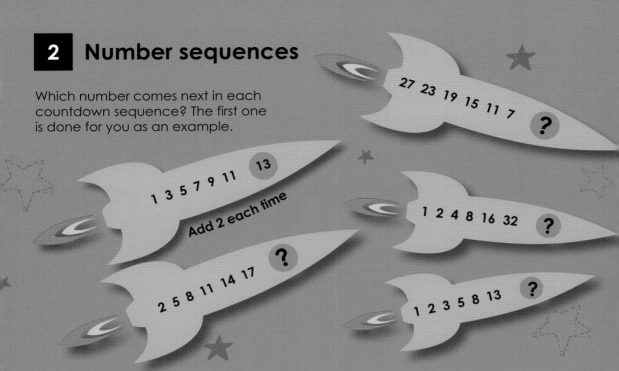

27 23 19 15 11 7 ?

1 3 5 7 9 11 13
Add 2 each time

2 5 8 11 14 17 ?

1 2 4 8 16 32 ?

1 2 3 5 8 13 ?

3 Brain chains

Start with the number on the left of each chain and follow each arrow in turn, applying each given math operation as you go. For example, in the first chain you begin with 9, subtract 2, multiply by 7, and then so on until you reach the end of the chain. Do this without making any written notes – see if you can solve the whole chain in your head. If you find this too easy, try to solve each chain in less than thirty seconds for an extra challenge!

9 — -2 — x7 — +3 — -4 — ÷8 — =?

17 — -14 — x4 — ÷3 — x12 — -11 — =?

12 — +16 — ÷4 — x5 — ÷7 — x8 — =?

Need help with solving these puzzles? Turn to pages 26 – 28 for helpful tips.

Find the Numbers

These challenges involve finding out which numbers will solve each problem. You can do this by working everything out on paper, or you can try just guessing. A guess that is not the right answer to a problem will often lead you a bit closer to the correct answer, so it's not always a bad way to start!

1 How old?

A mother is asked how old each of her three children is, and she says:

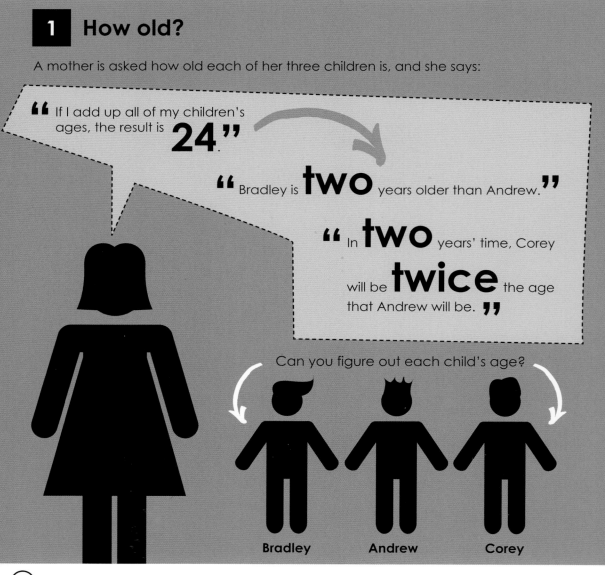

"If I add up all of my children's ages, the result is **24**".

"Bradley is **two** years older than Andrew."

"In **two** years' time, Corey will be **twice** the age that Andrew will be."

Can you figure out each child's age?

Bradley   Andrew   Corey

2 Street map

Look at the following drawing of three houses on a street, showing the number of each house. Can you tell which house each child lives in, based on the following clues?

- Five children live in the three houses pictured. Their names are Dan, Eliza, Frankie, Gabriela, and Hayden.

- If you add the house number where Eliza lives to the house number where Dan lives, you get 12.

- The total of the house numbers for Frankie, Hayden, and Dan is 19.

- The total of the house numbers for Hayden, Gabriela, Eliza, and Dan is 26.

- The total of the house numbers for Gabriela and Eliza is 14.

Dan   Eliza   Frankie   Gabriela   Hayden

5   7   9

3 Balloon bursting

Which of these balloons would you burst in order to leave only balloons that add up to the following totals?

44 35 19 18

13   4   5   10   17

Need help with solving these puzzles? Turn to pages 26 – 28 for helpful tips.

Amazing Numbers

You can do lots of clever things with numbers, from amazing your friends with sneaky math tricks to making up codes for sending secret messages.

1 Secret code

There are lots of ways to use numbers to hide secret messages. Perhaps the easiest way is to convert each letter to a number representing its position in the alphabet. A=1, B=2, and so on: Using this code, can you work out what this message says?

23	5	12	12		4	15	14	5

2 Super-secret code

To make your message more secure, you can change the numbers in some way. For example, you could number the alphabet backward so that Z=1 and A=26. Or you could reverse the digits, so instead of writing 13 for M you would write 31. With both of these changes – writing digits in reverse order and numbering letters from Z=1 to A=26 – what does this message say?

42	21	32	22

42	9	62	42	61	22	32

3 Ultra-secret code

In real-world codes, the way that a letter is encoded usually depends not just on the letter itself but on the letters that come before it, which can make it extremely difficult to crack a code. Here's an example of an ultra-secret code where each encoded number depends on the number before it! Let's start with just the super-secret code from number two. If we wanted to encode "ZOOM" we would get:

1	21	21	41

To make it ultra-secret, add the value of the previous number to each number. So we have 1, 21+1, 21+21, and 41+21:

1	22	42	62

Now each "O" has a different value, so that's why it's so hard for someone to guess what this message says! Now that you know how the code words, try decoding the message below. What day of the week is written here?

7	13	28	30	40	94	64

4 Math genius

Two's a crowd

Is 186 a multiple of 2? You probably already know how to tell if a number is a multiple of 2. It's easy: if the last digit is even (0, 2, 4, 6, 8), the number is a multiple of 2. So 186 is a multiple of 2 because 6 is even. If you want, you can also check by working out that 186 = 2 x 93.

Easy threesy

Is 186 a multiple of 3? You can answer this question with a quick trick: add the digits of a number (1 + 8 + 6 = 15 in this case), and if the answer is a multiple of 3, then so is the original number! 15 = 5 x 3, so 186 is a multiple of 3.

Four score

Is 516 a multiple of 4? Checking for multiples of 4 is a bit trickier. You need to find out if the last two digits make a number that's a multiple of 4. So you need to know your multiplication tables as far as 24 x 4 = 96. If the last two digits are a multiple of 4, then so is the full number. This means you can tell right away that 516 is a multiple of 4, because 16 is 4 x 4. Ignore any leading zeroes when you use this trick. So you know that 608 is a multiple of 4 because you read 08 as 8, and 8 is 2 x 4. You also need to keep in mind that 0 itself is also a multiple of 4, because 0 x 4 (no 4s!) is 0. That means 700 is also a multiple of 4.

Five star

Any number that ends in 5 or 0 is a multiple of 5. Easy!

The fix for six

How do you tell if a number is a multiple of 6? You just combine the tricks for spotting multiples of 2 and multiples of 3. So if it ends in an even number, and the digits add up to a multiple of 3, then it is also a multiple of 6.

You try it!

Solve these without a calculator, using the above tricks! They don't seem so impossible now, do they?

- Is 31,753 a multiple of 2?
- Is 938,676 a multiple of 3?
- Is 586,924 a multiple of 4?
- Is 18,484,830 a multiple of 5?
- Is 17,849,253 a multiple of 6?

Need help with solving these puzzles? Turn to pages 26 – 28 for helpful tips.

Open to Interpretation

Have you ever had a dream? Did you remember it? You can be really creative when you're dreaming, and there's no reason why you can't be just as creative when you're awake. It might be hard to think up ideas, but often all you need is something to get you started. Check out a few techniques that can help trigger wacky thoughts, and if you ever need to think up your own creative ideas, you can use these tricks to get going!

1 Hidden in plain sight

Look at the top left picture. It looks like a plain white rectangle with a small black dot in it. But is it really? It could easily be a picture of a polar bear in a snowstorm! All you can see is its nose. What creative explanations can you come up with for these other pictures? There are no wrong answers!

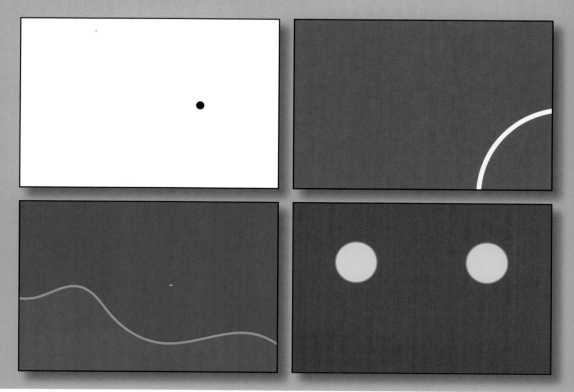

2 But what's it for?

Have you ever played idly with the items on your desk to see
what you can do with them? You can use an elastic band
and two pencils to make a catapult or turn a straw into a
peashooter.

These are fun ways to use items that are intended for completely different purposes.
Can you come up with alternative uses for each of the following sets of objects?

Remember, there are no official answers – it's up to you and your imagination!

1. A ruler and two erasers

2. A hair and a piece of sticky tape

3. A pencil case and some confetti

4. An orange, a lemon, and an apple

3 Acronyms

Sometimes we shorten common sequences of words by writing just their initials. These
are called acronyms, and it's particularly common with names of organizations.

For example, the United States is known as the U.S., and that's an acronym. It's
made up of the first letter of each word in the name. You can make up your own
acronyms, too, which only you know. For example, if RAT were an acronym related
to school, it could stand for Really Annoying Teacher! Here are some topics with
possible acronyms. Can you suggest what they might stand for?
It's entirely up to you!

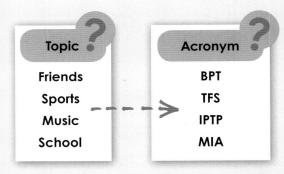

Topic ?	Acronym ?
Friends	BPT
Sports	TFS
Music	IPTP
School	MIA

Need help with solving these puzzles? Turn to pages 26 – 28 for helpful tips.

Riddles

A riddle is a word puzzle that you can solve with a clever interpretation of the question, sometimes by looking at different ways to use a word or an idea. You can solve these riddles by thinking carefully and looking out for clever tricks!

1 It's a riddle

Consider the saying...

" There's no 'I' in 'team.' "

This is sometimes used to show that everyone on a team should work together and not as an individual. It's witty because there really is no letter "i" in the word "team."

Riddles can sometimes be a bit like this, with multiple meanings. Here's an example:

"What word is always spelled incorrectly?"

Think about the exact meaning of this question. Is there a trick that makes it much easier than it first appears? If you're stuck, check the tips section. And if you're still stuck, take a look at the answer in the back before you try your hand at the other riddles on these pages!

2 Riddle me this

1. What is made by light and yet is always dark?

2. What goes up when rain comes down?

3. What word becomes shorter when you add two letters to it?

4. What has an eye but cannot see?

5. What can you catch but not throw back?

6. The more it dries, the wetter it becomes. What is it?

7. What is so delicate that just saying its name breaks it?

Need help with solving these puzzles? Turn to pages 26 – 28 for helpful tips.

Lateral Thinking

You've already tried out your logical puzzle-solving and number skills, and you've experimented with creative inventions. So how good are you at putting together your logical thoughts and creative ideas to solve seemingly impossible problems?

1 Clothes issues

1. Think about this problem:

If I pick up a scarf, how can I tie a knot in it without letting go of either end?

Does it sound impossible? It isn't. There is an easy solution that you could try out yourself with a scarf, a towel, a handkerchief, or any piece of material you can tie a knot in!

You're not allowed to let go at any time after you pick it up. But is there something you can do *before* you pick it up that would allow you to tie the knot?

You don't need to do anything to the scarf itself – it's all about the way you pick it up.

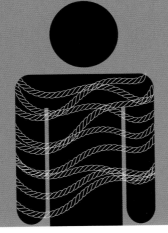

2. Here's another lateral-thinking puzzle involving clothing. You might come up with more than one solution, but there's a particularly simple way to solve it.

While wearing a pair of pants, how can I put my left hand into the right pocket and my right hand into the left pocket without crossing my arms?

If you think the answer is to put one hand behind your back, you'll probably find if you try it that you can't actually do that! There's at least one better method to discover.

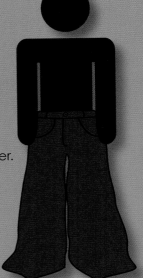

2 Thinking it through

All of these problems relate to time. How long will it take you to come up with answers?

Can you solve this? It sounds unlikely, but there's an easy explanation if you can find it.

1. The day before yesterday I was 8 years old. Next year I will be 11 years old. How can this be true?

This one is much sneakier! It might not be entirely to do with time.

2. Cowboy Bill rode into town on Friday. Then he rode out two days later on Friday. How is this possible?

Think about the extremes of Earth!

3. Between sunset and sunrise I got out of bed 120 times, and yet I managed to sleep over 8 hours between every single time that I got up. How can you explain that?

Here's another riddle that may or may not really be about time.

4. If I tell you that I know someone who predicts the future, how can I possibly be telling the truth?

Need help with solving these puzzles? Turn to pages 26 – 28 for helpful tips.

More Lateral Thinking

The lateral-thinking puzzles on these pages are designed to get your creative juices flowing. See what solutions you can come up with. There's not always just one right answer!

1 Lateral-thinking problems

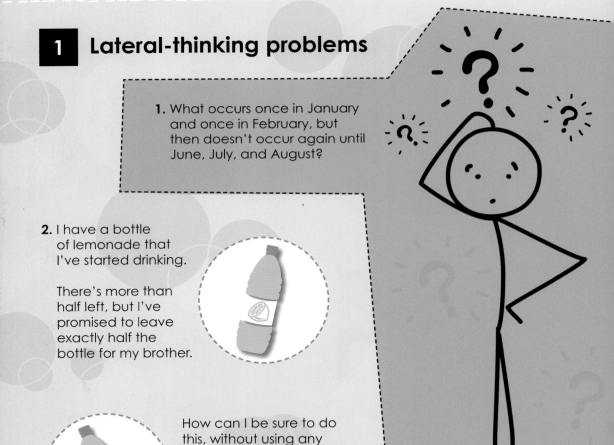

1. What occurs once in January and once in February, but then doesn't occur again until June, July, and August?

2. I have a bottle of lemonade that I've started drinking.

There's more than half left, but I've promised to leave exactly half the bottle for my brother.

How can I be sure to do this, without using any other item to measure it?

3. A proud father gave his son a pair of fancy pens, and a different proud father gave his son a set of four pens. Yet there were only four pens in total between both sons. How can this be true?

4. I'm holding a horse race, but I want to add a twist to the usual proceedings: the horse that comes in last will win. Of course, I don't want the race to go on forever, so what can I do to persuade the jockeys to ride normally?

5. My pet hamster has gotten stuck in a hole in the ground, and I can't reach in to get it out. Can you think of a simple way to get it out without hurting it?

Help!

6. If the Sea of Tranquility is on the Moon and the Black Sea is on Earth, on which planet is the Red Sea?

Ah, the Sea of Tranquility

Need help with solving these puzzles? Turn to pages 26 – 28 for helpful tips.

Even More Lateral Thinking

All of the lateral-thinking problems on these two pages have something to do with numbers. Some of them might even involve a bit of math, but a few have much sneakier answers!

1 Lateral-thinking problems

1. We can all agree that one comes before two, but how can two come after three and four before one?

2. Imagine that you place two identical coins on the table side by side so that they are touching.

   Now imagine that you hold the first coin down with your finger and roll the second coin all the way around the outside of the first coin, keeping the edges touching at all times.

   How many complete revolutions will the second coin have gone through by the time it gets back to where it started? Try to figure it out without using coins first.

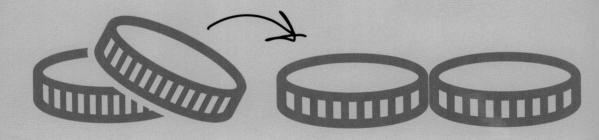

3. How can you stand over a bare concrete floor and drop an uncooked egg a distance of about 3 feet (1 meter) without it breaking? You cannot modify the egg in any way.

4. If Tom the tabby cat drinks precisely half of his saucer of milk every day, and none of the remaining milk evaporates or is removed, how long will it take him to finish a saucer containing a pint of milk?

5. If I pick up a spherical ball and mark any three points on it, what is the chance that all three points end up on the same half of the ball?

6. If I go for a walk in a forest, what is the farthest distance I can get from the edge of the forest? Write your answer as a fraction of the entire width of the forest.

Need help with solving these puzzles? Turn to pages 26 – 28 for helpful tips.

Language Games

If you've worked your way through the various puzzles in this book, you'll definitely be primed for some seriously creative thinking. Try a few more creative activities to test out your powers with words!

1 Fridge magnets

Imagine a fridge covered in magnetic letters that you can rearrange to make words.

The fridge magnets you see here display words instead of letters. What phrases, sentences, or stories can you make with these words?

The more creative the better!

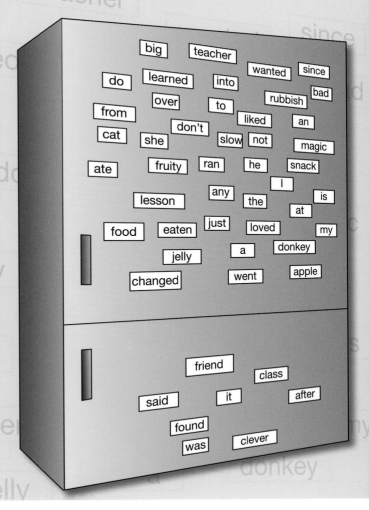

big teacher wanted since
do learned into rubbish bad
over to
from liked an
don't slow not
cat she magic
ate fruity ran he snack
I
any the is
lesson at
food eaten just loved my
jelly a donkey
changed went apple

friend class
said it after
found
was clever

2 Starting letters

Pick a letter of the alphabet. Can you think of the name of a country that starts with that letter? It's not so hard to think of Australia or Austria for A, for example, but can you do the same for every letter of the alphabet? There is at least one country beginning with every letter, except for X!

Here are some other lists you can try. You might not be able to find an item starting with every letter, but see how many you can manage!

Musical instruments

Movies

Fruits and vegetables

Boys' names

Girls' names

Five-letter words

Sports teams

Football players

Brand names

Shop names

TV shows

3 Explain this

You only need two dice to play this simple but creative game. Just roll both dice once for each column, and then explain the "Where, What, and Who" situation as creatively as you can! In each round, you'll get a place, an object, and a person or a group of people. Can you find an explanation for why that person or group has that object in that place? Some rolls will give easier tasks than others!

For example, if you roll a total of 7 the first time, the place is "at school." If you roll 3 the second time, the object is "a ruler." On your third roll, a 12 would give you "your best friend." So can you explain what your best friend would be doing with a ruler at school? That one is pretty easy, but chances are you'll come up with some that are much harder to explain!

	Dice roll 1 – Where?	Dice roll 2 – What?	Dice roll 3 – Who?
2	At a friend's house	A picture of the moon	A sports team
3	At your house	A ruler	Your family
4	On a bus	A football	The principal
5	In the park	A bat	A politician
6	At the mall	Your sports gear	A waiter
7	At school	A piece of fruit	A store clerk
8	On the football field	An alarm clock	An alien
9	On the playground	A sandwich	A famous sports star
10	At a museum	A measuring cup	A movie star
11	At a party	A baseball cap	Your teacher
12	At church	A sewing machine	Your best friend

Need help with solving these puzzles? Turn to pages 26 – 28 for helpful tips.

Helpful Tips

Page 5   It's Only Logical

Take a closer look at the words used in the question.

Pages 6 – 7

Numbers and Reasoning
Tricks with numbers

A good way to get the hang of these tricks is to work through them with different ages or numbers and see what happens in each case. Can you figure out how each different starting number gives you the same result after following the instructions?

Pouring problem

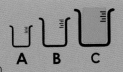

You start with 8 quarts in container C. If you pour as much as you can into B, you will have 5 quarts in B and 3 quarts in C. Now if you pour as much as you can from B into A, you will have 2 quarts in B. So you now know you can get an exact volume of 2 quarts, as well as 3, 5, and 8 quarts. You can also think about what's missing from each container. For example, if you had the 2 quarts in A, you could subtract exactly 1 quart from either B or C by filling up A.

River crossing

Remember that you can bring things across the river **and** bring them back again. And you can't leave the cat with any other item on either side of the river.

Pages 8 – 9

Number Manipulation
Number anagrams

If you are stuck, pick two random numbers and try adding or multiplying them. Now what do you need to do to get to the solution? Think about your multiplication tables. Is there something you can multiply to get closer to the result you need? What if you add two numbers, then multiply the answer?

Number sequences

These work like the example, except for the last one. There is a relationship here where each number is based on the two numbers before it. Can you see what it is?

Brain chains

If you find it difficult to remember the answers to each step as you go, try writing them down on a separate piece of paper.

Pages 10 – 11   Find the Numbers

How old?

Start by guessing at some of the children's ages and see how close to a valid answer you are. Then make small changes to your guesses until you find the solution.

Street map

Start with the clues that involve the least number of people, such as the last one. What are the possibilities for the house numbers of Gabriela and Eliza?

Page 11

Find the Numbers

Balloon bursting

Start by adding up all the balloons. Then figure out the total you would need to burst in each case. Once you've done that, you'll see that you only need to burst one balloon to end up with a total of 44, and that you'll need to burst more than one balloon to make the other totals.

Pages 12 – 13

Amazing Numbers

Super-secret code

You'll definitely find this easier if you write out the reverse-alphabet code first!

Ultra-secret code

Think about the addition the code uses. To undo the addition you must subtract something, and that something is the **decoded** number of each letter.

Math genius (You try it!)

All these questions can be answered with the rules you just learned.

Pages 14 – 15

Open to Interpretation

Hidden in plain sight

There are no correct answers here. If you can't think of anything, start by thinking of objects that are the same color as the background of the picture. For example, in the first picture the background is green. What can you think of that's green? Grass, perhaps? Aliens?

But what's it for?

Luckily for you, you can't possibly be wrong here, because there is no right answer! If you can't think of anything, try finding the actual items and playing around with them. Does anything come to mind now?

Acronyms

You don't need to think of something that fits all the letters right away. Try thinking of a word that starts with one of the letters – maybe B could be for "best" in the Friends topic. Then see if you can come up with ideas for the other letters. It doesn't matter if they sound silly!

Pages 16 – 17

Riddles

It's a riddle

Think carefully about what "incorrectly" means in this riddle.

Riddle me this

1) If you shine a light on an object, what can you see behind the object?
2) When it rains, what might someone put up?
3) What happens if you remove two letters from "shorter"?
4) Can you think of any objects that have an "eye"?
5) If you stay out in the rain without a coat, what might you catch?
6) What can you use to dry things?
7) When you talk in a quiet room, what do you break?

Page 18

Lateral Thinking

Clothes issues

1) If you can't let go of it, then can you do something with your arms before you pick it up?
2) This is physically very hard, if not impossible. So is there something you can do to the pants to make it easier?

Page 19 Lateral Thinking

Thinking it through

1) Think about what day it might be today. It's probably at the very start or the very end of the year, isn't it?
2) "Cowboy Bill" is capitalized because it's a name. What other words are capitalized?
3) Is there a place on Earth where it's dark for a very long time?
4) Take a very close look at the exact words in the question. What is definitely true in what I am saying?

Pages 20 – 21 More Lateral Thinking

Lateral-thinking problems

1) The solution to this has something to do with the words!
2) Do you have a lid for the bottle? If so, the bottle doesn't have to be standing upright, does it?
3) Imagine that you are one of the sons. Is it possible that the other son in the story could be related to you too?
4) If we assume that each jockey wants to win, what can the jockeys do to make sure that other horses finish before theirs?
5) Is there some way to fill in the hole without trapping the hamster at the same time?
6) Don't let the wording of the question fool you. It's designed to lead you toward an incorrect answer.

Pages 22 – 23 Even More Lateral Thinking

Lateral-thinking problems

1) Notice that in this question the numbers are written as words. Could that be important?
2) Once the second coin has traveled halfway around the first one, you might expect it to have done half a revolution. But are you sure?
3) Read the question carefully. Make sure you understand exactly what is being asked!
4) If half is always left, what effect will this have on the answer to the question?

5) Imagine that you're holding a ball in your hands. Think about three points on it. Can you picture how they could all be on one half of the ball?
6) You know that a fraction tells you how much of something you have, which in this case is how far across the width of the forest you've traveled. For example, you could go a quarter of the way into the forest. At that point, how far would you be from the opposite edge? And at what point in are you farthest from either edge of the forest?

Pages 24 – 25 Language Games

Fridge magnets

If you're short of inspiration, just put your finger on the page without looking and take that as your starting word! What can come next?

Starting letters

If you find this tricky, get some friends to help. Activities like this are often easier to do with a group. That's because you'll all have different bits of knowledge, and the sum of everything you know together is usually more than what any of you knows on your own.

Explain this!

Your explanation doesn't have to make logical sense. It can be as ridiculous as you like! This game is best played with friends – see who can think up the funniest explanation!

Answers

Page 5

It's Only Logical

What occurs once in a minute, twice in a moment, but not once in a thousand years? The letter "m."

Pages 6 – 7

Numbers and Reasoning

Tricks with numbers

You can see how the first trick works by using a label for your age. Let's say your age is "a." If we double your age, we get "a x 2." Now we add 6, which gives "a x 2 + 6." Then we divide it by 2, which means we take half of the "a x 2," which is of course just "a" again, and half of the 6, which is 3. So we now

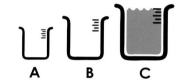

have "a + 3." Then we subtract your age again, which leaves us with just 3. And that's how it works! You can come up with similar mathematical routines to make your own number tricks.

The second trick relies on the fact that any multiple of 9 has digits that also add up to a multiple of 9. You can check this for yourself, from 1 x 9 through to 10 x 9, giving 9, 18, 27, 36, 45, 54, 63, 72, 81, 90. We ask you to think of a number from 1 to 9 and add 1, so you're really thinking of a number from 2 to 10. As you can see, when any of these numbers is multiplied by 9, the answer has two digits that add up to 9. So when you add on 6, you are certain to get 15.

Pouring problem

The solution requires 7 steps:
- Pour C into B so you now have A = 0, B = 5, C = 3
- Pour B into A for 3, 2, 3
- Pour A into C for 0, 2, 6
- Pour B into A for 2, 0, 6
- Pour C into B for 2, 5, 1
- Pour B into A for 3, 4, 1
- Pour A into C for 0, 4, 4

A   B   C

River crossing

First bring over the cat, which can't be left with the dog or the cat food. Then go back and get either the dog or the cat food. Here's the trick: when you get to the far bank again, **bring the cat back to the first side**. Then you can bring over the dog or the cat food, whichever you left behind. Go back a third time to get the cat. Done!

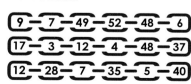

Pages 8 – 9

Number Manipulation

Number anagrams

$19 = 7 \times 2 + 5$ $13 = 3 \times 4 + 7 - 6$
$37 = 5 \times 7 + 2$ $15 = 3 \times 6 + 4 - 7$
$49 = (5 + 2) \times 7$ $34 = (3 + 7) \times 4 - 6$

(The brackets mean that you add the 5 and 2 first before multiplying by 7.)

Number sequences

2 5 8 11 14 17 20
(add 3 each time)

27 23 19 15 11 7 3
(subtract 4 each time)

1 2 4 8 16 32 64
(multiply by 2 each time)

1 2 3 5 8 13 21 (add the previous two numbers each time)

Brain chains

9 — 7 — 49 — 52 — 48 — 6

17 — 3 — 12 — 4 — 48 — 37

12 — 28 — 7 — 35 — 5 — 40

Pages 10–11 Find the Numbers

How old?

Andrew is 5, Bradley is 7, and Corey is 12.

Street map

Let's call the children by their initials: D, E, F, G, and H. We know that E + D = 12, so since we have the numbers 5, 7, and 9 to choose from, this means that either E = 5 and D = 7, or E = 7 and D = 5. We also know that E + G = 14, so either E = 5 and G = 9, or E = 9 and G = 5. But we already know that E can only be 5 or 7, so it must be E = 5 and G = 9. This also means that D = 7. So that's three children assigned to houses! Next, we know that H + G + E + D = 26, and since we know the values of G, E, and D, we can be sure that H = 5. Finally, we know that F + H + D = 19, and since we already know D and H, this means F = 7. So the answer is: Eliza and Hayden – No. 5
Dan and Frankie – No. 7
Gabriela – No. 9

Balloon bursting

- 44 – burst 5
- 35 – burst 4 and 10
- 19 – burst 13 and 17
- 18 – burst 4, 10, and 17

Pages 12–13 Amazing Numbers

Secret code
WELL DONE

Super-secret code
CODE CRACKED

Ultra-secret code This is more complex to decode because you need to do some subtraction! Start with the first letter, 7, which we know is T (since T = 7, U = 6, V = 5, W = 4, X = 3, Y = 2, and Z = 1). Then subtract the 7 from the next number, 13, to get 6. We know that 6 is U. Next, subtract the **decoded number,** 6, from the next number, 28, to get 22, E. Keep going until you can read the whole word: TUESDAY.

Math genius (You try it!)
- **A multiple of 2?** No, because it doesn't end in an even number.
- **A multiple of 3?** Yes, because the digits add up to 39, which is a multiple of 3. If you're not sure, you can add the digits of 39 to get 12, which you know is 4 x 3.
- **A multiple of 4?** Yes, because 24 is 6 x 4. $\sqrt{a^2} = |a|$
- **A multiple of 5?** Yes, because it ends in a 0 or a 5.
- **A multiple of 6?** No, because it does not end in an even number, even though it is actually a multiple of 3.

Page 15 Open to Interpretation

But what's it for?

There are no correct answers for this, but here are some ideas!

1) Make a seesaw with one eraser and the ruler, then put the other eraser on one end of the seesaw, and punch down on the opposite end to send it flying across the room!
2) Make a trap to see if anyone's been in your room. Tape across a closed door would be obvious, but if you tape a hair across your door instead, then if someone goes into your room, they'll dislodge the hair without noticing they've set off your trap!
3) Put the confetti in the pencil case and then balance it on top of a door to surprise someone… but only do this with a cloth pencil case!
4) You could try juggling the fruit!

Acronyms

There are no correct answers for this either, but here are some possibilities to get you going if you can't think of anything!

Acronym	Topic	Suggestion
BPT	Friends	Birthday Party Tonight
TFS	Sports	This Football Stinks
IPTP	Music	I Play The Piano
MIA	School	Math Is Awesome

Page 16 Riddles

It's a riddle

The word "incorrectly" is always spelled "incorrectly," isn't it?

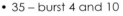

Page 17 Riddles

Riddle me this

1. A shadow! You might also think up other answers.
2. An umbrella, and again you can probably think of other answers related to rain.
3. "Short" becomes "shorter" when you add the two letters "er"!
4. A needle. Or you might have said a potato, and you can find other answers to this, too.
5. A cold. Or perhaps something that is about to destroy itself in some way, but a cold is the classic answer to this riddle!
6. A towel!
7. Silence! If you speak in a quiet room, you "break" the silence.

Pages 18 – 19

Lateral Thinking

Clothes issues

1. Before you pick up the scarf, fold your arms so that your right hand is resting on top of your left arm. Grab the scarf with both hands and uncross your arms – and it will be knotted!
2. Put the pants on backward, so the right and left pockets swap positions!

Thinking it through

1. It's January 1st today, and my birthday is on December 31st. I'm 9 years old today, but the day before yesterday, December 30th, I was still 8. At the end of this year, on December 31st, I will turn 10, and the year after ("next year") I will have my 11th birthday on December 31st.
2. Cowboy Bill's **horse's name** is Friday!
3. I must be living in or near the Arctic or Antarctic, where there is no daylight in winter! The sun never rises during this time.
4. I say that my friend predicts the future, but I'm not saying that my friend predicts the future **accurately** – I'm just saying that he or she **predicts** it.

Pages 20 – 21 More Lateral Thinking

Lateral-thinking problems

1. It's the letter "u."
2. If you put the bottle flat on its side (with the lid on!), you can easily see whether it is still more than half full. You can keep checking in this way until the bottle is precisely half full.
3. One father was the son of the other father, so he just passed on the two pens his own father had already given him, plus two more of his own.
4. You get the jockeys to swap horses with one other. They will still want their own horses to win, so they will try to finish ahead of their horses by riding normally.
5. One method is to pour in sand (slowly!) until the hamster can climb out by itself.
6. Earth! The question is written to trick you into thinking the answer is Mars, since Mars is known as the Red Planet due to its color.

Pages 22 – 23 Even More Lateral Thinking

Lateral-thinking problems

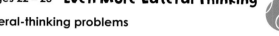

1. They do in a dictionary! When sorted alphabetically, the words four, one, three, and two are in this order.
2. The outer coin will perform two full revolutions.
3. You simply catch the egg after dropping it.
4. It will take him forever, since he always leaves half – and if he always leaves half, then he can't ever finish it!
5. It works – try it out! Your points will always show up on one half of the ball.
6. Half the width of the forest is the farthest you can go. Once you've walked more than halfway into the forest, you'll start getting closer to the far edge instead!

Index

About the Author

Dr. Gareth Moore is the author of a wide range of puzzle and brain-training books for both children and adults, including *The Kids' Book of Puzzles*, *The Mammoth Book of Brain Games*, and *The Rough Guide Book of Brain Training*. He is also the founder of daily brain training site **www.BrainedUp.com**. He earned his Ph.D from Cambridge University (UK) in the field of computer speech recognition; teaching machines to understand spoken words.